Lift Every Voice and Sing

Lift Every Voice and Sing

James Weldon Johnson

Illustrations by Elizabeth Catlett

INTRODUCTION BY JIM HASKINS

Walker and Company
New York

This edition published in the United States of America in 1993
by Walker Publishing Company, Inc.

Published simultaneously in Canada by Thomas Allen & Son
Canada, Limited, Markham, Ontario

Library of Congress Cataloging-in-Publication Data
Johnson, James Weldon, 1871–1938.
   Lift every voice and sing / James Weldon Johnson; woodcuts by
Elizabeth Catlett.
       p. cm.
   Includes music for voice and piano.
   Summary: An illustrated version of the song that has come to be
considered the African American national anthem.
   ISBN 0-8027-8250-7
   1. Songs, English—United States—Texts. [1. Afro-Americans—
Songs and music. 2. Songs.] I. Catlett, Elizabeth, 1919– ill.
II. Title.
PZ8.3.J6334Li   1993
782.42164′026′8—dc20   92-27333
                                                        CIP
ISBN 0-8027-8251-5 (REIN)   AC

Book design by Georg Brewer
Printed in the United States of America

10 9 8 7 6 5 4 3 2

Introduction

▼

I was in the fourth grade when I learned "Lift Ev'ry Voice and Sing." I remember having some difficulty with both the tune and the words. Like the part in "The Star Spangled Banner" that begins "and the rockets red glare," there are some high notes in "Lift Ev'ry Voice and Sing." Some of us found it hard to lift our voices as high as the tune required. The words were harder to learn than those of the other songs we sang because there were no choruses. Every line of the song had new words. But we knew it was important to learn both the tune and the words because "Lift Ev'ry Voice and Sing" was *our* song. In fact, we called it the Negro National Anthem.

In those days, just as in the days when James Weldon Johnson and his brother, J. Rosamond Johnson, wrote the song, African-Americans were not accepted as full-fledged Americans. In Demopolis, Alabama, where I grew up, and in other parts of the South, we were not allowed to vote, to eat in white restaurants, or to drink from the same public water fountains as whites. We could not swim in the public pool or enter the public library. Most textbooks only talked about Negroes, as we were called then, as slaves.

What was nice about "Lift Ev'ry Voice and Sing" was that it was honest about all the suffering black Americans had undergone but celebrated our triumph over that suffering. In spite of slavery, in spite of segregation, in spite of all the pain of being black in white America, we Negroes continued to have faith that things would get better. Our parents taught us to be proud of who we were and to be the best we could be. Our teachers taught us that our history was far more than just slavery and that we could help make things better for ourselves.

Both James Weldon Johnson (1871–1938) and his younger brother, J. Rosamond (1873–1954), were teachers when they wrote the words and music for "Lift Ev'ry Voice and Sing." Born in Jacksonville, Florida, they were bright and talented young men. James loved to write and attended Atlanta University. J. Rosamond had great musical gifts and studied at the New England Conservatory of Music. With their career opportunities severely restricted by racial discrimination, both returned to Jacksonville after college to teach in the public schools. James Weldon served as a public school principal, and J. Rosamond as supervisor of music for the public schools. They got together and wrote "Lift Ev'ry Voice and Sing" for schoolchildren to sing at a celebration of the birthday of Abraham Lincoln on February 12, 1900.

Not long afterward, the brothers moved to New York City, where they formed a highly successful songwriting team with another man, Bob Cole. Later, James Weldon sought a more active role in bettering the lives of black Americans. He went to work for the National Association for the Advancement of Colored People (NAACP) and became the first Negro executive secretary of that organization. Founded by blacks and whites, the NAACP worked to end segregation and to promote the rights of black people.

Johnson believed that an uplifting song would be a way for black people to express their pride in who they were. He remembered the song he and his brother had written some twenty years earlier. With the support of the NAACP, he began to encourage the singing of the song as a Negro national anthem. In the years since, it has been sung by millions of black people. And both its words and its music are as inspiring today as they were when I learned them in fourth grade—and probably as they were to those children in Jacksonville, Florida, nearly a century ago. African-Americans today enjoy the rights, if not all the opportunities, of full-fledged citizens. But "Lift Ev'ry Voice and Sing" reminds us of how far we traveled to win them.

Like James Weldon Johnson, the artist Elizabeth Catlett (1919–) is an activist in the cause of civil rights for black people. The granddaughter of North Carolina slaves, she was born and raised in Washington, D.C. She wanted to be a painter, but when she applied to an all-white art school, Carnegie Institute of Technology, she was refused entry. She went to the all-black Howard University instead and, on graduating, enrolled in the graduate school of the University of Iowa. She was the first student to receive a Master of Fine Arts degree from that school.

After graduation, Catlett supported herself by teaching art at various black colleges. In addition to painting, she also did printmaking. Many of her prints are linocuts, made by carving a picture into a block of linoleum, inking the block, and then pressing it onto a piece of paper. Linocuts are much like woodcuts, but linoleum is less expensive and easier to work with. Both Catlett's paintings and her prints are often about poor black men and women who led hard lives but endured with strength and dignity. The strong lines in the prints that illustrate this book help to convey the strength of the people she depicts.

These prints were made in 1946 and 1947. In 1947, for both personal and professional reasons, Catlett moved to Mexico. She was tired of fighting racism at every turn, and she believed her art would find a wider audience. Happily for her, she enjoyed wide acceptance and high regard in Mexico, where she became a citizen in 1962. After Catlett moved to Mexico, she turned to sculpture, but her subjects—ordinary, hardworking people—have remained the same.

It is amazing how well her work illustrates the words of "Lift Ev'ry Voice and Sing," for the prints were done completely independent of the song. Her bold lines tell the story of a people often abused and downtrodden, but enduring and strong, able to "face the rising sun" each day and to "march on till victory is won."

—Jim Haskins

Lift Every Voice and Sing

LINOCUT *13 x 19cm*   *1947*

Lift ev'ry voice and sing

Till earth and heaven ring,

*Ring with the harmonies of
Liberty;*

LINOCUT 15 x 22.5cm 1947

Let our rejoicing rise

High as the listening skies,

Let it resound loud as the
rolling sea.

LINOCUT   16 x 16cm   1946

*Sing a song full of the faith
that the dark past has
taught us,*

*Sing a song full of the hope
that the present has
brought us,*

LINOCUT   18 x 23cm   1946

Facing the rising sun of our new day begun

Let us march on till victory is won.

LINOCUT   15 x 12cm   1946

Stony the road we trod,

Bitter the chastening rod,

*Felt in the days when hope
unborn had died;*

LINOCUT   23 x 15.5cm   1947

Yet with a steady beat,

Have not our weary feet

Come to the place for which
our fathers sighed?

LINOCUT 15 x 21.5cm 1946

*We have come over a way
that with tears has been
watered,*

*We have come, treading our
path through the blood of
the slaughtered,*

LINOCUT   15.5 x 23cm   1946

Out from the gloomy past,

Till now we stand at last

Where the white gleam of our bright star is cast.

LINOCUT   15.5 x 23cm   1946

God of our weary years,

God of our silent tears,

Thou who has brought us thus far on the way:

LINOCUT 10 x 13.25cm 1947

Thou who has by Thy might

Led us into the light,

Keep us forever in the path,
we pray.

LINOCUT   15 x 11cm   1946

Lest our feet stray from the places, Our God, where we met Thee,

Lest, our hearts drunk with the wine of the world, we forget Thee;

LINOCUT 15.5 x 23cm 1947

*Shadowed beneath Thy
   hand,*

May we forever stand.

True to our GOD,

True to our native land.

When Elizabeth Catlett was awarded a Julius Rosenwald Foundation grant in the 1940s, she saw the opportunity to work on a project "for the people." She decided to focus on black women and went to Mexico to begin her series of paintings, prints, and sculpture, from which these linocuts were taken.

Elizabeth Catlett's original captions to the art

Lift Ev'ry Voice and Sing

Lyrics by
James Weldon Johnson

Music by
J. Rosamond Johnson

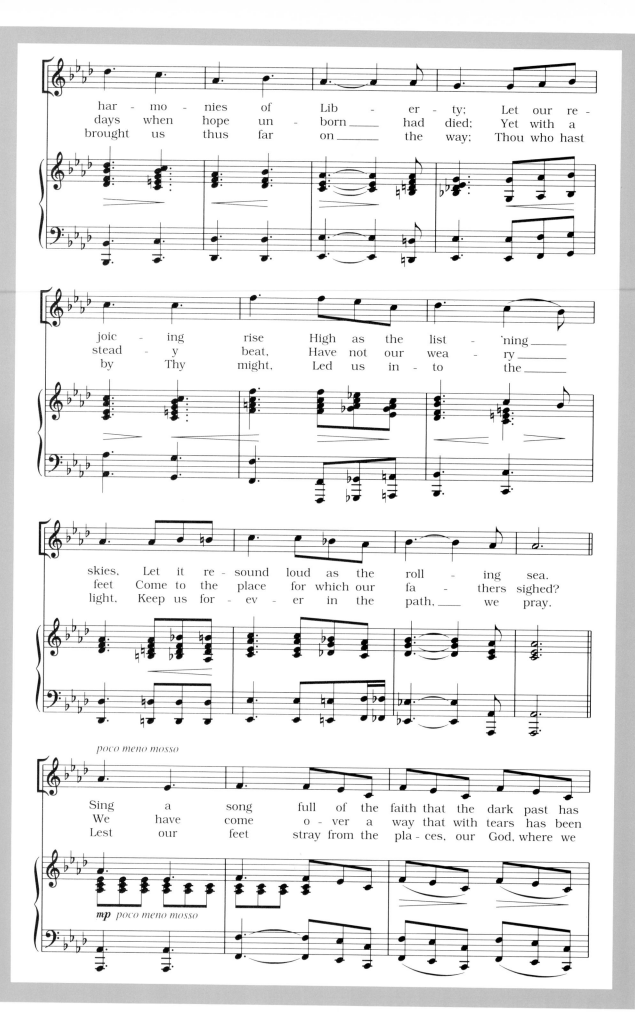

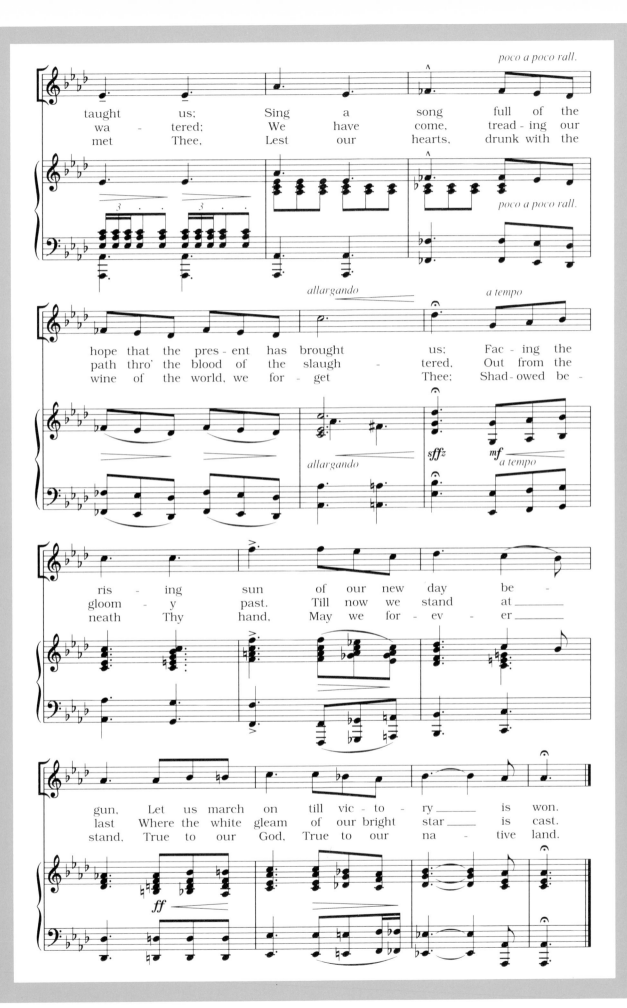

Notes on the book

The display typography is set in Fantastik, composed by
All American Photolettering, Incorporated, of
Ridgewood, New York.

The text typography is set in ITC Veljovic Bold and ITC
Veljovic Bold Ital, composed by Linoprint Composition
Company, Incorporated, of New York City, New York.

The sheet music was set by Computa-A-Chart of
Nashville, Tennessee.

The interior and jacket of the book were printed by
Eusey Press of Leominster, Massachusetts, on 100-pound
Lustro Dull Cream, manufactured by
S. D. Warren Company.

The book was bound by Book Press of Brattleboro,
Vermont, with Kennett Cloth by Industrial Coatings
Group, on the spine, and Rainbow Antique Paper by
Ecological Fibers, on the sides.

Book production coordinated by Our House.

Book art direction and design by Georg Brewer.

The text of this book was printed in two flat colors
throughout the interior, with two flat colors, one tinted
varnish, and one clear matt varnish on the jacket. This
book is self ended and bound using .088 binders boards.

The inks used in printing this book were soybean-oil
based, and the binder boards are made of
100 percent recycled material.